Culinary Arts Ltd.

Gourmet Mustards

HOW TO MAKE
AND COOK WITH THEM

Helene Sawyer

Mustard

Original cover art by Robert Francis
Editorial Staff: Cheryl Long
Heather Kibbey
Cynthia Fischborn

Copyright © 1987
By Helene Sawyer

Library of Congress Cataloging-in-Publication Data

Sawyer, Helene, date.
Gourmet Mustards.

Includes index.
1. Cookery (Mustard) 2. Mustard (Condiment) I. Title.
TX819.M87S28 1987 641.6'384 87-9223
ISBN 0-914667-07-6 (paper bound)
ISBN 0-914667-09-2 (comb bound)

Printed in the United States of America

Published by:
Culinary Arts Ltd.
P.O. Box 2157
Lake Oswego, Oregon 97035

Books by Culinary Arts Ltd.:
How To Make Danish Fruit Liqueurs
How To Make A World Of Liqueurs
How To Make And Cook With Gourmet Vinegars
Gourmet Mustards: How To Make And Cook With Them

Publisher's catalog available upon request.

TABLE OF CONTENTS

INTRODUCTION

Ah! Christmas 1982! Less than one month on a new job, no money in my pocket for gifts... it was time to hit the kitchen again for a new creation. Jams and jellies I'd done before, as too taco sauce, chow chow, zucchini bread, etc. This year it had to be different. Why not mustards? I've used mustard, not only on sandwiches but also in cooking, in my salad dressings and sauces. I love mustards! My cabinets were full of herbs and spices, so I immediately began experimenting and came up with four different recipes. My very "lucky" friends got all four flavors.

Some of the remarks that came back from the tasting were music to my ears. Everything from "Lime Mustard??? You've got to be kidding! What would you use that on?" to "Oh my, whatever you did to this one, could you mass-produce it? You have a marketable product."

The first question was easy enough to answer, the second really made me think. I decided to try my hand at marketing gourmet mustard for one year. Now, over four years later, I am having the time of my life, running my company, Chateau d'Helene, specializing in the production of gourmet mustards and mustard mixes.

This world of ours has given us the fruits to create the finest wines and liqueurs, the herbs and spices to create any taste we can conceive for our palates, including the tiny mustard seed, often thought of as only good for making a condiment to use on sandwiches or as a spice for pickling. For the real truth is: mustard is a spice, along with cinnamon, cloves and nutmeg. That opens up new horizons!

With this book, I share my knowledge of how to make gourmet mustards for home use or for gifts, as well as how to use these mustards in your everyday cooking for that extra flair.

With mustards as with fine wines, the development of the palate is an adventure. I hope you will enjoy this experience as much as I have.

Helene Sawyer

ABOUT THE AUTHOR

Like many successful food writers, Helene Sawyer has a passion for good food. Her career began, not in the kitchen, but in the science laboratory, as a Nuclear Medicine Technologist. Passion and science met, and produced a successful gourmet mustard manufacturing company, Chateau d'Helene, in Canby, Oregon. Each year since 1983, Helene and her good friend Viki have produced thousands of jars and packages of gourmet mustards in an exciting array of flavors.

ACKNOWLEDGMENTS

To Robert, Bruce, and Joy Word for years of taste testing my creations. Some made it; some did not. For giving me a location to start my company and moral support at each step of the way. To Leslie for introducing me to the world of fine food I now enjoy and for the hours she let me help around the deli to get started. To all my other friends, too numerous to mention, for help with creating and smoothing out recipes. To the new friends I'm making, Cheryl Long, Heather Kibbey and Cynthia Fischborn, who are helping to make a dream come true.

"A tale without love is like beef without mustard: an insipid dish."

Anatole France, French humorist.

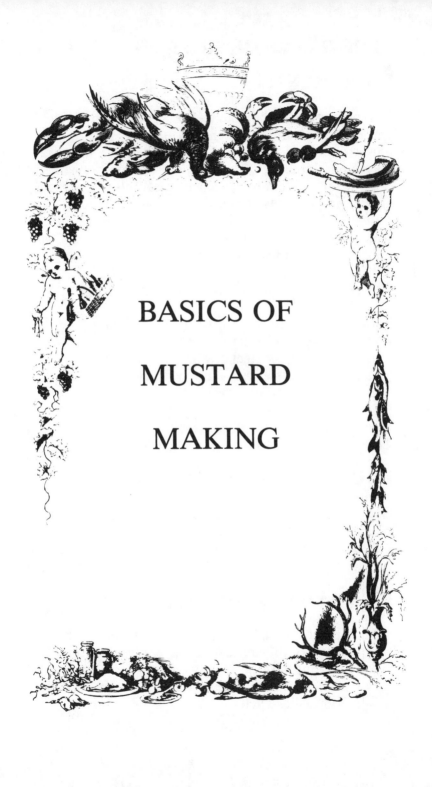

BASICS OF

MUSTARD

MAKING

THE BASICS OF MUSTARD MAKING

EQUIPMENT:

You will probably be able to find all the equipment
you need in your own kitchen. One basic rule in
mustard making is to avoid contact between mustard
paste and aluminum. The presence of vinegar, wine or
other acidic materials can leach metal molecules from
aluminum pans. Use only plastic, glass, enameled or
stainless steel utensils for making your mustards. For
storage and aging of mustards, use only glass jars with
tight-fitting plastic or enamel-lined lids.

MUSTARD MAKING EQUIPMENT:

Plastic or stainless steel measuring spoons
Plastic or stainless steel spoons for mixing
Plastic or stainless steel strainer or colander
Plastic, stainless steel or glass measuring cups, ¼- to
   2-cup size
Plastic or rubber spatula
Blender or food processor
Cheesecloth for garni bags and straining

EQUIPMENT FOR STORING:

Glass jars in 4-, 6- or 8-ounce sizes
Plastic or enamel-lined metal lids
Labels
Fabric, yarn or ribbon to decorate jars for gift giving

PREPARATION OF EQUIPMENT:

All equipment used for mustard making should be
completely free of grease or other contamination.
Wash all items with hot soapy water, then rinse with
very hot, clear water, or put your equipment through
a full dishwasher cycle.

MUSTARDS:

For superb gourmet mustards, you must start with good quality products. The true Dijon mustard uses the "black mustard seed". This "black" seed is actually brown and, in fact, the "white" variety is really yellow in color. Black mustard seed is much smaller and more pungent than the white. White mustard has almost no volatile oil, therefore dry mustard is usually a combination of both black and white seeds. White mustard seed is used in pickles, relish, or recipes such as corned beef, where "whole seed" is required.

HERBS, SPICES, FRUITS, VEGETABLES, WINES:

All the ingredients used should be top quality. When fresh herbs are required, choose leaves with no wilted or browned edges. Fresh herbs should be washed and patted dry before chopping. When using dried herbs, take a look at the product and see that it appears fresh. If dried herbs have been around for awhile, they start to lose their deep color and appear "washed out". Herbs will lose the oils in their leaves as they age, especially if they have not been properly sealed and stored. It's these oils that will be released in the mustard recipe, giving the ultimate flavor.

If you have your own herb garden, as I have had, it doesn't take long to go out and snip a tablespoon of lemon thyme to add to your mustard recipe. A housewarming gift of Lemon Thyme Mustard is even more special when the recipient knows you also grew the herb.

When using spices, again use the freshest possible. A jar of cinnamon, for example, that's been sitting three years on your shelf has lost a lot of its punch. Replace your spices frequently, so that they don't become old and flavorless.

9

The same rule applies to fruit: choose the brightest, plumpest and juiciest. Limes, lemons and oranges are good examples. The skin, or zest, of the citrus fruit is where the highly flavored oils are. So avoid fruits with any brown spots, and reap the full flavor.

Some recipes call for vegetables, such as onions or shallots. Again, they need to be bruise-free, plump and juicy so that all their flavors will be released into the recipe.

If a recipe calls for wine, be sure it is of good quality. I use a dry white wine, a vermouth, in most of my recipes calling for "white wine". For red wines, I prefer a dry, full-bodied red. The Italian and Spanish reds are good, as are the French Bordeaux. For sherries and champagne, choose dry, rather than sweet.

AGING, STORING, AND SHELF LIFE:

Remember that by crushing the mustard seed, you have just released its volatile oils. Therefore your newly prepared mustard is at its most pungent state, hot and bitey. It's quite like Chinese hot mustard that is made up just before it is served. At this point, if you prefer this degree of pungency, refrigerate your mustard when you have finished transferring it to a clean sterile jar. Refrigeration retards the decrease in pungency. For a milder mustard, allow it to age, unrefrigerated. My recommendation is to place the mustard in your jar and seal it with a tight-fitting enamel-lined lid. Store it in a cool, dark place and wait 3 to 8 weeks, or longer if you still prefer a little less bite. At the point you find the pungency or degree of hotness that you like, refrigerate your jar of mustard.

Some of the mustard recipes in this book start with a prepared Dijon-style mustard base, with other flavors added. The base may be either the Basic Dijon-style Mustard from my recipe, or a ready-made Dijon from the store. Once you use either of these bases to create a new mustard flavor, it must be aged at room temperature for at least two weeks to allow the flavors to mingle. Taste after aging to evaluate the pungency. If you prefer a milder mustard, age another two weeks, then test again. Once the mustard reaches the level of mildness you enjoy, refrigerate.

No matter what its age, mustard will not grow mold, mildew or harmful bacteria. It may dry out, lose its flavor and turn dark brown from oxidation, but even so, it is safe to eat. If it dries out, just add wine or vinegar to reconstitute.

The shelf life of mustard is indefinite. This is one food that is so versatile. You can make it up a couple of months before giving it as a gift, or whip up a batch at the last minute, provided you give aging instructions to the recipient.

EQUIVALENT MEASURES

1 tsp.	=	5 ml.
1 Tbsp.	=	15 ml.
1 fluid ounce	=	29.56 ml.
1 fluid cup	=	236 ml.
1 ounce	=	28.35 grams or .028 kg.
1 pound	=	454 grams or .454 kg.

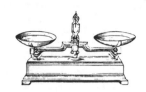

MUSTARD HISTORY AND FACTS

In the United States, the present consumption of mustard is greater than every other spice except pepper.

Mustard was known to have been an ingredient in Indian curry thousands of years ago.

*The word **"moutarde"** may be used on French mustard labels only if the mustard is made with black mustard seed.*

In France some mustards are aged in wooden casks, as is wine.

A survey in France in 1812 revealed that 93 different kinds of mustard were available.

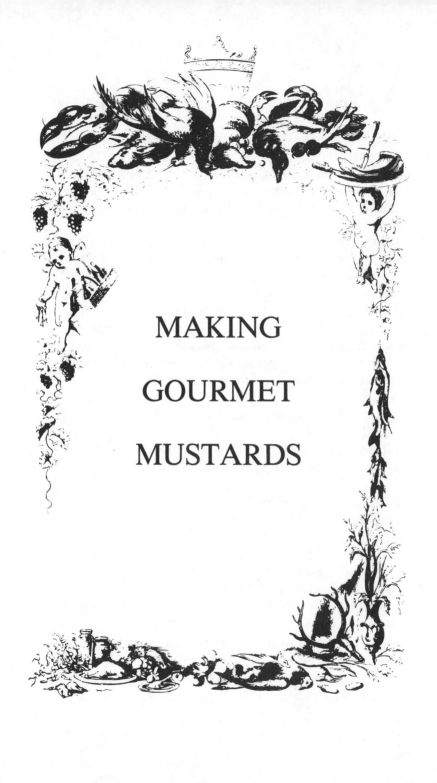

MAKING

GOURMET

MUSTARDS

With the directions and recipes in this book you will be able to fill your pantry with a selection of gourmet mustards. You will soon be replacing regular prepared mustard with some of your favorite gourmet mustards. You will also be able to create some of your own original gourmet mustards with the information contained in this book. I hope you receive as much enjoyment in the creative process as I have. When making mustards remember that using vinegar instead of water in a mustard recipe weakens the enzyme reaction and produces a milder, less biting mustard. Water may be called for when a **very hot** mustard is desired such as in **CHINESE HOT MUSTARD**. Thus you can control the hotness by the ingredients used as well as aging. Salt and vinegar or wine actually help preserve the strength of the mustard so that it retains its flavor for a very long time. Adding that touch of gourmet mustard gives foods that subtle extra taste that good cooks strive for. Your friends will ask for your secrets. If you're like me, you will share most of your recipes. But I like to also keep a few for my own special secret.

I may shatter a lot of beliefs when I say that the inexpensive, bright yellow, "hot dog style" mustard should not be considered the "basic" mustard for cooking purposes. Oh, it tastes great on hot dogs. In fact, nothing else would be quite right. But for cooking, the Dijon-style mustard is far superior, because of its ability to enhance so many flavors.

The gourmet mustards and some of the special food recipes in this book are very giftable. Give a special mustard as a gift and tie a recipe using it to the container. Enjoy!

BASIC DIJON-STYLE MUSTARD

A culinary classic! Makes 1½ cups.

2 cups dry white wine
1 large onion, chopped
3 cloves garlic, pressed
1 cup (4 oz.) dry mustard
3 Tbsp. honey
1 Tbsp. oil
2 tsp. salt

Combine wine, onion and garlic in a saucepan. Heat to boiling and simmer 5 minutes. Cool and discard strained solids. Add this liquid to dry mustard, stirring constantly until smooth. Blend in honey, oil and salt. Return to saucepan (have hankies ready or hold face away from steam) and heat slowly until thickened, stirring constantly. Cool; place in covered jar. Age in cool, dark place 2 to 8 weeks, depending upon pungency desired, then refrigerate.

Now the fun and creativity begins! Let your cooking skills take you into a new world by just adding a few simple ingredients to your finished Dijon-style mustard. Or for an easy head start, buy a jar of good Dijon-style mustard and start your creativity there. See how simple, yet elegant, the following recipes can be.

HONEY DIJON MUSTARD

A real sweety: hot and sweet. Makes 1 cup.

1 cup honey
1 cup **DIJON-STYLE MUSTARD**

Combine ingredients. Transfer to a jar with a tight-fitting lid. Age in a cool dark place 2 to 8 weeks, then refrigerate.

HERBED MUSTARDS

This recipe is as unlimited as your imagination. Vary herbs for your own special flavor. Makes 1 cup.

1 Tbsp.of one of the following dried herbs: Herbs de Provence, tarragon, dill weed, lemon thyme, rosemary **or** basil.
1 Tbsp. dry vermouth
1 cup **DIJON-STYLE MUSTARD**

Combine the herb and the vermouth in a medium bowl and let stand 20 minutes. Gradually mix in mustard. Transfer to jar with tight-fitting lid. Store in a cool dark place for 2 weeks, then refrigerate.

THREE HERBS MUSTARD

This is a delicately flavored blend. Makes 1½ cups.

¼ cup fresh parsley **or** 2 Tbsp. dried.
¼ cup fresh tarragon leaves **or** 2 Tbsp. dried
¼ cup fresh dill weed **or** 2 Tbsp. dried
1 cup **DIJON-STYLE MUSTARD**

When using fresh herbs, place in a food processor and mix to finely chop. Add mustard and blend until smooth and creamy. When using dried herbs, mix herbs in a medium bowl and stir in mustard until well blended. Transfer to a jar with tight-fitting lid. Store in a cool dark place for 2 weeks, then refrigerate.

LEMON, LIME, ORANGE OR LEMON-LIME MUSTARD

A fresh, zesty mustard that is great in sauce recipes. Makes 1 cup.

1 cup **DIJON-STYLE MUSTARD**
1 Tbsp. fresh lemon, lime **or** orange juice
2 tsp. honey
Grated peel, (zest), of lemon, lime **or** orange.

Mix all ingredients in a medium bowl. Transfer to jar with a tight-fitting lid. Store in a cool dark place for 2 weeks, then refrigerate.

SHALLOT MUSTARD

Lightly flavored with onion and garlic. Makes 1 cup.

3 large shallots, chopped
1 cup **DIJON-STYLE MUSTARD**

Combine ingredients. Transfer to a jar with a tight-fitting lid. Age in a cool dark place for 2 to 8 weeks, then refrigerate.

JALAPEÑO MUSTARD

Zippy, and for the brave! Makes 1 cup.

2 Tbsp. chopped canned jalapeño peppers (save liquid)
1 Tbsp. reserved jalapeño liquid
1 cup **DIJON-STYLE MUSTARD**

Mix peppers and juice with mustard. Transfer to a jar with a tight-fitting lid. Age in a cool dark place for 2 to 8 weeks, then refrigerate.

GREEN PEPPERCORN MUSTARD

Delicious on pork chops, poached seafood, or to spice up mayonnaise. Makes 2 cups.

½ cup hot water
¼ cup whole yellow mustard seed
1 cup dry mustard
½ cup dry vermouth
¼ cup honey
1 tsp. dried tarragon leaves, crumbled
1 tsp. salt
⅛ tsp. ground cloves
⅛ tsp. ground allspice
⅛ cup green peppercorns, drained

Combine water and mustard seed in small bowl and let stand one hour. Drain well. Transfer mustard seed to a food processor or a blender. Add remaining ingredients except peppercorns and purée, stopping machine several times to scrape down sides of container. (Mixture will be coarse.) Add peppercorns and blend. Transfer to a jar with a tight-fitting lid. Age in a cool dark place for 2 to 8 weeks, then refrigerate.

APRICOT MUSTARD

An exotic mustard that's great with stout cheeses. Makes 1½ cups.

1 cup **SWEET 'N' HOT MUSTARD**
½ cup apricot jam

Mix together in a bowl. Transfer to a jar with a tight-fitting lid. Age in a cool dark place for 2 to 8 weeks, then refrigerate.

SWEET 'N' HOT MUSTARD

Great with pâtés, ham, meat loaf and pork. Or try some mixed with peanut butter for a real flavor pick-up. Makes 2 cups.

3 Tbsp. anise seed, crushed
1½ cups dry mustard
¾ cup firmly packed brown sugar
¾ cup apple cider vinegar
1½ tsp. salt
½ cup oil

Process anise seed in blender or food processor until crushed, about 3 minutes. Add mustard, sugar, vinegar and salt; mix well. Stop frequently to scrape down the sides of the work bowl. With the machine running, add oil in a slow, steady stream and blend until the mixture is the consistency of mayonnaise. Transfer to a jar with a tight-fitting lid. Age in a cool dark place for 2 to 8 weeks, then refrigerate.

HORSERADISH-LOVERS MUSTARD

Requests for a horseradish mustard recipe outnumber all others two to one! Makes about 1½ cups.

1 cup dry mustard
½ cup powdered sugar
½ tsp. salt
½ cup white wine vinegar
¼ cup oil
1 Tbsp. fresh lemon juice
¼ tsp. grated lemon peel (zest)
5 Tbsp. prepared horseradish

Put all ingredients in food processor or blender and mix well. Stop freqently to scrape down sides of work bowl. Transfer to jar with a tight-fitting lid. Age in a cool dark place 2 to 8 weeks, then refrigerate.

CHAMPAGNE MUSTARD

A very "giftable" mustard. I recommend aging this one 3 to 4 months for a more delicate flavor. Makes 1½ cups.

1 cup dry mustard
½ cup powdered sugar
½ tsp. salt
6 oz. flat champagne
1 Tbsp. fresh lemon juice

Place all ingredients in a blender or food processor and mix until smooth. Stop frequently to scrape down sides. Transfer to a jar with a tight-fitting lid. Age in a cool dark place 3 to 4 months, then refrigerate.

Variation: For **CHAMPAGNE HONEY MUSTARD**, substitute ½ cup honey for the powdered sugar in the recipe above.

RED WINE MUSTARD

Another chance to let your imagination go! This hearty, herb-flavored recipe makes a mustard with great Italian style. Makes 2 cups.

1 cup dry mustard
½ cup brown sugar
½ cup red wine, (dry Italian **or** Cabernet preferred)
1 Tbsp. of one of the following dried herbs: rosemary, oregano, marjoram **or** basil*
½ tsp. salt
⅓ cup oil

Put all ingredients, except oil, in food processor work bowl or blender. Combine until creamy. With machine running, add oil through feed tube in a slow but steady stream. Blend until the consistency of mayonnaise. Stop machine frequently and scrape down sides of bowl. Pour into jar with tight-fitting lid. Age in a cool dark place 2 to 8 weeks, then refrigerate.

*NOTE: You may combine any of these herbs to measure 1 tablespoon total for an Italian treat.

BAVARIAN BROWN MUSTARD

This is a grainy, Bavarian-style mustard. Makes 1½ cups.

½ cup whole brown mustard seed
¾ cup dry sherry
1 cup dry mustard
¼ cup brown sugar
¼ tsp. salt

Combine mustard seed and sherry in a medium bowl and let stand 2 to 3 hours. Transfer mixture to food processor or blender and blend until almost smooth, (mustard will be grainy). Add dry mustard, sugar, and salt and blend well. Place in jar with a tight-fitting lid. Age in a cool dark place 2 to 8 weeks. Store in a cool dark place.

Tip: For creamier mustard, add more sherry until that consistency is reached.

ENGLISH PUB MUSTARD

In Britain this is made up fresh each day to serve with bangers, cold cuts, meat pies and chops. Remember, dry mustard when first mixed with liquid releases its oil and is at its hottest. From there, it starts to cool down. Makes 1½ cups.

1 cup dry mustard
½ cup firmly packed brown sugar
1 tsp. salt
¼ tsp. turmeric
6 oz. flat beer **or** ale

Put mustard, sugar, salt and turmeric in a food processor or blender and mix well. With the machine running, add beer through feed tube slowly but in a steady stream. Blend until smooth and creamy, stopping machine to scrape down sides of work bowl frequently. Transfer to jar with a tight-fitting lid. Age in a cool dark place for 2 weeks. Store in refrigerator.

CHINESE HOT MUSTARD

A nippy tradition for dipping egg rolls or fried shrimp. Makes 1 cup.

1 cup dry mustard
¾ cup water

Mix ingredients in a small bowl. Transfer to jar with a tight-fitting lid. Age in a cool dark place for 2 weeks. Refrigerate.

Tip: For the nippiest **CHINESE HOT MUSTARD**, eliminate the aging period and serve or refrigerate immediately.

HOT SWEDISH-STYLE MUSTARD

A hot and spicy Scandinavian favorite. Wonderful on all types of cold cuts, wieners and sausages. This mustard thickens as it sits overnight. Makes 1½ cups.

3 eggs
¼ cup packed brown sugar
½ cup honey
⅓ cup apple cider **or** juice
⅓ cup apple cider vinegar
⅔ cup dry mustard
½ tsp. salt
¼ tsp. ground cardamom
¼ tsp. ground cloves
¼ tsp. ground mace, (optional)
¼ tsp. ground cinnamon

Beat eggs in a large non-aluminum saucepan. Add remaining ingredients and mix well. Cook over low heat, stirring constantly until mixture thickens, about 10 minutes. Let cool. Transfer to jar with tight-fitting lid. Age in a cool dark place 2 to 8 weeks, then refrigerate.

HINTS AND TIPS ABOUT MUSTARD

Remember that dry mustard is a spice and can be used along with cloves, cinnamon or allspice.

No matter what its age, mustard will **NEVER** grow mold, mildew or harmful bacteria. Mustard may dry out, lose its flavor and change to a dark brown color in its old age, but it will not harm anyone.

Attention dieters: A gourmet food you can enjoy is mustard. Mustard averages about 5 calories a teaspoon.

Mustard is an emulsifier. Add enough mustard to a salad dressing and it will help hold the oil and vinegar together. It can also minimize the possibility of curdling when used in a Hollandaise sauce.

Mix in a bit of any flavored Dijon-style mustard with your next egg dish. It gives it a wonderful flavor boost.

Add any flavored Dijon-style mustard, to taste, to your favorite potato salad recipe. A great flavor pickup and change.

A different "French Dip" sandwich? Just dip sandwich into your mustard vinaigrette instead of *au jus*.

Spread one of your favorite gourmet mustards on your next grilled cheese or peanut butter sandwich for real flavor punch.

When making your favorite quiche, spread a thin layer of flavored Dijon-style mustard on the crust before filling. It will help prevent a soggy crust and add zip to the flavor.

COOKING

WITH

GOURMET

MUSTARDS

t is not necessary to be an experienced cook to use gourmet mustards. I certainly was not when I first began. Just remember that mustard is a spice as well as a condiment. Begin to add some mustard to some of your favorite recipes, using some of my recipes as guides.

Here are several tips to remember as you begin to cook with mustard. If you want the pungency of mustard, add it at the end of the cooking period and keep the heat low (do not boil). When, however, the flavor of the mustard is important and not its pungency, then higher temperatures and longer cooking or baking times are not a problem.

If you are cooking with dry mustard, you should know that it is similiar to curry in hotness. It is a spice as well, and can be used nicely along with cloves, cinnamon or allspice. You may cook with dry or prepared mustards. Each has its own character and flavors. Don't be afraid to experiment a bit; that's the way I built my collection of recipes.

CHEESE FRITTERS

The cheese is soft and warm inside, but crispy on the outside. What a terrific combo! Serve with **HORSERADISH MUSTARD SAUCE.** *Serves 8 as an appetizer, 4 as an entrée.*

1 lb. Gruyère **or** Emmentaler **or** Swiss cheese
1 cup flour
salt and pepper, to taste
1 egg
1¼ cup dry white wine, warmed
2 egg whites, stiffly beaten
2 Tbsp. **TARRAGON MUSTARD**
oil for deep frying

Sift flour into a bowl and season with salt and pepper. Make a well in the center of of the flour and break the egg into it. Gradually work the egg into the flour, then slowly stir in about ¾ cup of wine. Beat well, then stir in the remaining wine and the mustard. Fold in the egg whites.

Cut cheese into 8 pieces, each ½" x ½" x 3". Dip into the fritter batter. Fry in very hot deep oil until golden brown on both sides. Serve immediately.

SHRIMP IN DILLED MAYONNAISE

This splendid recipe is perfect for a buffet or open house menu. It may be served as either a salad or an appetizer. Serves 6 to 8.

2 Tbsp. oil
2 lbs. medium shrimp in shell
3 to 4 Tbsp. fresh dill, minced, **or** 1½ to 2 Tbsp. dried dill weed
2 Tbsp. fresh parsley leaves, minced
½ cup mayonnaise
1 tsp. **LIME, DILL, LEMON, LEMON-LIME, SHALLOT, CHAMPAGNE** *or* **HORSERADISH LOVERS MUSTARD**
½ tsp. salt
1 small onion, minced
8 lettuce leaves, when served as salad

Over medium-high heat, sauté shrimp in small batches in heated oil until opaque, about 3 minutes. Remove shrimp, drain and cool; then peel and halve lengthwise.

Combine the next 6 ingredients, mixing well. Add shrimp, gently stir to coat each one. Transfer to bowl with tight-fitting lid. Chill 6 hours or overnight, stirring occasionally. Serve on lettuce leaves as a salad, or with crackers as an appetizer.

SHRIMP REMOULADE

This recipe is incredibly good! Outstanding as an appetizer or salad. Serves 4 to 6.

1½ lbs. cooked shrimp
2 Tbsp. **LIME** *or* **LEMON** *or* **LEMON-LIME MUSTARD**
1 tsp. paprika
1 tsp. seafood seasoning
½ cup mayonnaise
1 celery heart, minced
1 Tbsp. tarragon vinegar
salt and pepper, to taste
dash of cayenne pepper

Combine all ingredients and toss with shrimp. Chill overnight in refrigerator. Pile into lettuce-lined bowl.*
Serve as an appetizer with homemade crispy rounds of french bread.

*NOTE: For eye-appeal, red leaf lettuce makes a beautiful presentation.

B-DEVILED TOMATOES

A festive and tasty topping for tomatoes. Serves 8.

4 large tomatoes, cut in half
pinch of salt
1 Tbsp. **ANY HERBED MUSTARD**
1 Tbsp. chopped green onion
2 Tbsp. chopped celery
2 Tbsp. chopped green pepper
2 Tbsp. melted butter *or* margarine *or* **MUSTARD BUTTER**

Preheat oven to 425 ° F. Place tomatoes, cut side up, in a baking dish. Sprinkle with salt. Spread cut side of tomato with mustard. Combine next 4 ingredients; spoon onto tomatoes. Bake for 10 minutes. Serve hot or warm.   29

BEEF TERIYAKI

An easy and quick snack. Make this a day ahead so flavors will blend. Makes 18 appetizers.

½ cup soy sauce
¼ cup dry sherry
2 Tbsp. pineapple juice
2 Tbsp. brown sugar
2 tsp. dry mustard
1 Tbsp. **DIJON-STYLE** *or* **SWEET 'N' HOT MUSTARD**
4 cloves garlic, minced
1½ lbs. beef tenderloin (partially frozen)

Combine soy sauce, sherry, sugar, mustards and garlic. Cut partially frozen meat into thin strips. Thaw meat completely. Add meat to marinade and marinate overnight. Thread meat strips accordian-style on small skewers. Grill over hot coals to desired doneness, about 5 to 7 minutes. Turn and baste with marinade frequently.

ARTICHOKE BYTES

An elegant, sizzling hot appetizer. Makes 24.

1 (14 oz.) can artichoke bottoms
½ cup Italian dressing, regular **or** low-calorie
1 Tbsp. **HERBES DE PROVENCE** *or* **ANY HERBED MUSTARD**
⅛ tsp. garlic powder
6 slices boiled ham, cut in 1"x4" strips
¼ lb. mozzarella cheese, cut in ½" cubes

Drain artichokes. Combine next 3 ingredients then add artichokes. Marinate 4 to 6 hours; drain. Place cheese in well of artichoke bottom. Wrap with strip of ham; secure with wooden toothpick. Bake for 10 minutes in a 300° F oven.

BEER AND CHEESE SPREAD

Beer, cheese and gourmet mustard are a winning combination! the variety lies in the type of mustard used. Makes about 3 cups.

2 cups sharp cheddar cheese, shredded
2 cups Swiss cheese, shredded
1 tsp. Worcestershire sauce
2 Tbsp. **ENGLISH PUB** *or* **JALAPEÑO** *or* **HOT SWEDISH-STYLE MUSTARD**
1 tsp. dry mustard
1 clove garlic, minced
½ to ⅔ cup flat beer

Have cheese at room temperature. Combine cheeses, Worcestershire sauce, mustards and garlic. Beat in enough beer to bring to spreading consistency.

Tip: If you have a food processor, this recipe is a snap.

MUSTARD BUTTER

Make a variety of these to serve your guests. Good spread on hot breads and appetizers.

½ cup, (1 stick) sweet butter
1 to 6 tsp. **ANY GOURMET MUSTARD**
dash Worcestershire sauce
lemon juice, to taste
chopped parsley **or** dill weed **or** chives

Allow butter to soften slightly. Combine mustard, Worcesterhire and lemon juice with butter, mix well. Place on plastic wrap. Shape into a log or ball. Refrigerate a bit if too soft. Roll log in garnish of choice. Wrap in fresh piece of plastic wrap and refrigerate until needed.

MARINATED COLE SLAW

Make this a day ahead so the flavors have a chance to blend. Serves 4 to 6.

½ red cabbage, shredded
½ green cabbage, shredded
1 red onion, diced
1 bell pepper, red **or** green, diced
1 carrot, grated
¼ cup sugar

Mix all ingredients together in large bowl. Cover. Make dressing.

COLE SLAW DRESSING

½ cup white wine vinegar*
¼ cup oil
1 tsp. salt
1 Tbsp. **BASIC DIJON-STYLE MUSTARD**
1 tsp. pepper

Boil all ingredients in saucepan for 3 minutes. Stir well. Add to vegetable slaw mixture, re-cover and refrigerate overnight.

*NOTE: If you use Marsha Peters Johnson's cookbook, **HOW TO MAKE AND COOK WITH GOURMET VINEGARS**, the variations are limitless. Select your favorite vinegar and mustard combinations or try mine. Lime Vinegar and **LIME MUSTARD** *or* Apricot with Allspice Vinegar and **SWEET 'N' HOT MUSTARD** *or* any mixed herbed vinegar with a matching **HERBED MUSTARD**.

PIQUANT SHELL PASTA

Very tangy when first made, yet flavors mellow as it chills. An excellent pasta salad! Serves 4 to 8.

8 oz. shell pasta, cooked, drained and cooled
3 ribs celery, chopped
8 green onions, chopped
1 carrot, shredded
1 long green chili, peeled and chopped
1 cup steamed broccoli flowerettes
1 red bell pepper, chopped
½ cup oil
3 Tbsp. Basil, Cilantro, Tarragon **or** Basic Herbed Vinegar*
1 Tbsp. **BASIL, TARRAGON, HERBES DE PROVENCE, THREE HERBS, RED WINE** *or* **GREEN PEPPERCORN MUSTARD**
salt and pepper, to taste
½ cup fresh Parmesan cheese, grated

Combine first 7 ingredients in large bowl. In separate bowl, combine remaining ingredients to make dressing. Toss with salad. Chill before serving.

CREAMY MUSTARD SALAD DRESSING

A smooth, creamy dressing that has so many delicious variations. Simply vary the mustard for a new flavor experience. Makes ⅓ cup.

¼ cup mayonnaise
1 Tbsp. half and half **or** light cream
½ tsp. dry mustard
¼ tsp. salt
⅛ tsp. pepper
1 Tbsp. any **DIJON-BASED MUSTARD**

In a small bowl, mix all ingredients thoroughly. Chill and serve.

PIQUANT MUSTARD SALAD DRESSING

Try this on a spinach salad for raves. Vary the mustard and vinegars for tasty variations. Makes 2 cups.

¼ cup sugar
3 Tbsp. **DIJON-STYLE MUSTARD**
1 tsp. salt, optional
½ tsp. pepper
½ tsp. garlic powder
1 tsp. Worcestershire sauce
2 Tbsp. lemon juice
1 cup oil
½ cup white wine vinegar

Mix all ingredients except oil and vinegar in a small bowl. Add a small amount of the oil to make a paste. Put remaining oil and vinegar into a blender; add paste and blend briefly until mixed. Serve.

HELENE'S POPPY SEED DRESSING

This is one of the best dressings I've ever tasted. Hope you agree! Makes 1¾ cups.

½ cup honey
⅓ cup tarragon vinegar
1 tsp. salt
½ tsp. dry mustard
1 Tbsp. **TARRAGON MUSTARD**
1 large shallot, minced
1 cup oil
1 Tbsp. poppy seeds

Combine first 6 ingredients in a blender; blend briefly. Turn blender on LOW, remove lid and pour in oil in a slow steady stream. Turn off blender, add poppy seeds, and pulse once or twice to mix. Store in refrigerator; use within 2 weeks.

CREAM OF BROCCOLI SOUP

A hearty and wonderful soup. Serves 4 to 6.

½ lb. bacon, fried crisp and crumbled
1 large onion, chopped
2 Tbsp. flour
1 large head of broccoli, chopped
2 (12-oz.) cans chicken broth
2 cups half and half **or** light cream
3 Tbsp. **DILL** *or* **CHAMPAGNE** *or* **SHALLOT** *or* **HONEY DIJON** *or* **JALAPEÑO MUSTARD**

In a large soup pot fry bacon crisp. Remove bacon, drain off drippings, reserving 2 tablespoons. Crumble bacon and set aside. Add reserved bacon drippings to soup pot, add onions and sauté until golden and transparent. Add flour, whisking constantly; then whisk in chicken broth. Add broccoli to mixture and cook over medium heat for 10 minutes. Turn heat to low and gradually add half and half, stirring constantly for another 10 minutes. Remove from heat; add mustard, salt, pepper and bacon. Serve hot.

CREAM OF MUSTARD SOUP

A superb and unusual soup that is rich with cream and has a delicate flavor. Serves 6 to 12.

2 (12-oz.) cans chicken broth **or** 24 oz. homemade broth
2½ cups Chablis-style white wine
2 Tbsp. butter
1 Tbsp. flour
1 Tbsp. dry mustard
2 egg yolks
1 cup heavy cream
2 Tbsp. **HERBES DE PROVENCE MUSTARD**
white pepper, to taste
3 green onions, chopped for garnish

Pour chicken broth and wine into saucepan and bring to a boil. Reduce heat; keep warm over low heat.

In a small bowl, beat egg yolks with pepper and cream; set aside. In soup pot, over low heat, melt butter and whisk in the flour and dry mustard (to make a roux), stirring for a minute. Slowly pour in the hot chicken broth mixture, whisking until smooth and thickened. Add a little of the thickened chicken broth mixture to the eggs and cream, and stir. Then pour the cream mixture into the soup pot, stirring constantly. Remove pan from heat and add the mustard. Garnish with green onions.

Variations: Substitute a different mustard for a new flavor experience. Try: **LEMON MUSTARD**, with a slice of lemon garnish. **LIME MUSTARD**, with a slice of lime garnish. **BASIL MUSTARD**, with a fresh leaf of basil. **DILL MUSTARD** , with a sprinkle of dill weed. **TARRAGON MUSTARD**, with fresh tarragon leaves. **CHAMPAGNE MUSTARD**, with cold strips of chicken breast. **GREEN PEPPERCORN MUSTARD**, with a few green peppercorns. **SHALLOT MUSTARD**, with cold baby shrimp.

THE SOUP OF NAPOLEON

Soup with an elegant French touch! Serves 6.

½ cup butter
2 lbs. onions, finely chopped
3 cups white burgundy wine
1 can (12-oz.) chicken broth
8 oz. grated Emmentaler cheese
3 Tbsp. **HERBES DE PROVENCE** *or* **DILL** *or*
  TARRAGON *or* **LEMON THYME MUSTARD**
2 cups croutons

Sauté onions in butter over low heat until tender but
not brown, in a large soup pot. Whirl cooked onions
in blender, then return to pot. Stir in wine and
chicken broth. Cook until soup is very hot, but not
boiling. Reduce heat and add cheese, a handful at a
time, stirring until melted. Add mustard.

Place croutons in bottom of each bowl, add soup.
Garnish with a dab of butter and one of the
following: chopped parsley, dill weed, tarragon or
lemon slice.

EGGS HELENE

*Dave Bergman at Thadius' Pantry in the Sellwood
area of Portland, Oregon, named this recipe for me
and added it to the menu. Serves 2.*

6 eggs
1 Tbsp. **HERBES DE PROVENCE MUSTARD**
2 Tbsp. butter
salt and pepper, to taste
¼ cup sharp cheddar cheese, grated

In bowl, scramble eggs, mustard, salt and pepper.
Melt butter in sauté pan over low heat. Add egg
mixture and cook to desired doneness. Add cheese and
serve.

FRITTATA
(ITALIAN STYLE BAKED OMELETTE)

This is wonderful! Present with sauce and Italian sausage. Serves 4 to 6.

9 eggs
4 Tbsp. **HERBES DE PROVENCE MUSTARD**
1 tsp. dry mustard
3 Tbsp. butter
1 (6-oz.) jar marinated artichoke hearts
6 fresh mushrooms, thickly sliced
3 green onions, 1″ diagonally cut
½ cup broccoli flowerettes
20 Chinese snow peas

Preheat oven to 375°F. Steam broccoli, snow peas and green onions conventionally 5 minutes. Or microwave, covered, 1 minute on HIGH (100% power). Set vegetables aside.

In a large bowl scramble eggs and mustards. In ovenproof skillet, melt butter, then pour in egg mixture. Add all vegetables, and place skillet in oven. Bake 45 to 55 minutes, uncovered, until eggs have set in middle. Make sauce while eggs are baking.

FRITTATA SAUCE
Makes about 1 cup.

3 egg yolks
1 stick unsalted butter, cut into 16 pats
1 cup grated Swiss cheese
2 Tbsp. **HERBES DE PROVENCE MUSTARD**

Place egg yolks in top of double boiler, over simmering, not boiling, water, whisking constantly until lemon colored and thickened. Be sure heat is not too high as yolks will curdle. Add butter, 2 pats at a time, whisking until melted, until all butter has been added. Add cheese a handful at a time stirring until melted, then add mustard. Remove from heat and pour over frittata.

YORKSHIRE CHEESE PUDDING

A variation on a classic side dish to roast beef. Serve in place of potatoes or rice. Serves 4 to 6.

2 eggs
1 Tbsp. **LEMON** *or* **LIME** *or* **BASIC DIJON-STYLE MUSTARD**
3 Tbsp. bacon or roast beef drippings, warmed
1 cup milk
1 cup flour
1 tsp. dry mustard
1 cup finely grated Gruyère cheese

Preheat oven to 450°F. Beat eggs in a medium bowl until very thick and lemon colored. Add mustard. Gradually add milk, then drippings, blending thoroughly. Add flour and dry mustard; beat until smooth. Fold in half the cheese. Pour mixture into a well-greased 1-quart baking dish, and top with the remaining cheese. Bake for 25 minutes or until golden brown. Serve immediately.

CHEDDAR CHEESE PUDDING

An easy and wonderful change of pace. Serves 4 as a light entrée or side dish.

½ cup cheddar cheese, preferably English white cheddar
½ cup Colby cheese
2¼ cups milk
1 Tbsp. any herbed mustard
1 tsp. dry mustard
2 cups fresh white bread crumbs
2 eggs, lightly beaten

Preheat oven to 375°F. Bring milk to a boil and pour over bread crumbs. Add cheese and mustards, then stir in eggs. Pour mixture into a deep-dish pie plate or casserole and bake in preheated oven for about 35 minutes or until golden brown and well risen. **39**

HERBED CHEESE AND SAUSAGE QUICHE

This is my favorite quiche. I hope you enjoy it as much as I do. Serves 6 to 8.

2 Tbsp. vegetable oil
½ lb. Italian sausage, ground (or slip meat out of casings)
1 large shallot, minced
7 egg whites
3 eggs
3 Tbsp. **HERBES DE PROVENCE MUSTARD**
½ tsp. dry mustard
1 cup half and half **or** light cream
½ cup Monterey Jack cheese, grated
½ cup sharp cheddar cheese, grated
1 tsp. baking powder
1 tsp. salt (optional)
½ tsp. white pepper
1 baked 9-inch deep-dish pie shell

Preheat oven to 425°F. Heat oil in large skillet over medium heat. Add sausage and shallot. Sauté until sausage is cooked through, about 3 to 5 minutes. Discard excess oil. Set mixture aside.

Whisk or beat egg whites in large bowl until frothy. In another bowl combine 3 eggs, mustards, half and half, cheese, baking powder, salt and pepper. Stir mixture into beaten egg whites.

Sprinkle sausage and shallot mixture over bottom of pastry. Pour egg white mixture over sausage. Bake 15 minutes. Reduce oven temperature to 300°F and continue baking until puffed and golden brown, about 40 minutes. Let cool on metal rack 10 minutes before slicing. Serve hot.

LA GRANDE QUICHE

This recipe was given to me by a very dear friend. It's an elegant dish for a special brunch or late supper. Serves 6 to 8.

¼ cup unsalted butter
1 small onion, finely chopped
2 eggs
1 Tbsp. **TARRAGON** *or* **HERBES DE PROVENCE** *or* **THREE HERBS MUSTARD**
1½ cups half and half **or** light cream
¼ cup Parmesan cheese
1 tsp. nutmeg, freshly grated
salt and pepper, to taste
¼ cup broccoli, chopped, blanched and well drained
2 Tbsp. unsalted butter, melted
½ tsp. dried basil, crumbled
¼ tsp. Worcestershire sauce
¼ tsp. dried Fines Herbes, crumbled
⅛ tsp. coriander
⅛ tsp. cinnamon
⅛ tsp. garlic powder
⅛ tsp. ground cumin
dash paprika
1 baked 9-inch deep-dish pie shell
2 Tbsp. Parmesan cheese, freshly grated
1½ cups smoked turkey breast, cut into ½" cubes
2 cups Swiss cheese

Position rack in center of oven. Preheat oven to 350°F. Melt ¼ cup butter in small skillet over low heat. Add onion and sauté until soft and transparent. Set aside.

Beat eggs until light and fluffy. Stir in mustard, half and half, ¼ cup Parmesan, nutmeg, salt and pepper. Combine well.

Combine broccoli, 2 tablespoons melted butter, basil, Worcestershire, Fines Herbes, coriander, cinnamon,

41

garlic powder, cumin and paprika in a medium bowl
and toss lightly until thoroughly mixed.

Sprinkle pie shell with 2 tablespoons Parmesan, add
sautéed onion, spreading evenly. Arrange broccoli
mixture over onion, top with turkey. Cover completely
with Swiss cheese. Pour in egg mixture to just below
rim of pie shell. Bake until quiche is set, about 50
minutes (filling will be slightly sticky). Let stand 15
minutes before serving.

DILLED ALBACORE QUICHE

*This easy-to-make quiche is a great luncheon or dinner
entrée. Serves 6 to 8.*

2 (7-oz.) cans albacore tuna, water pack, (reserve
   liquid)
2 eggs, beaten
½ cup sour cream
3 Tbsp. mayonnaise
2 Tbsp. **DILL** *or* **HERBES DE PROVENCE** *or*
   SHALLOT *or* **JALAPEÑO** *or* **LEMON** *or* **LIME
   MUSTARD**
3 dashes cayenne pepper, or to taste
1 cup Emmentaler **or** German Swiss cheese, shredded
2 Tbsp. green onion, finely chopped
2 large dill pickles, finely chopped
½ tsp. dried dill weed
1 baked 9-inch deep-dish pie shell

Preheat oven to 325 ° F. Add water, if necessary to
reserved albacore liquid to make ¼ cup. Pour into
large bowl, stir in beaten eggs, sour cream,
mayonnaise, mustard, and cayenne.

Add albacore tuna. Blend in Swiss cheese, onion,
pickle and dill weed. Pour mixture into baked pie
shell. Bake until set, about 40 minutes. Cool on rack
10 minutes before slicing. Serve warm.

OREGON SEAFOOD BROIL

Fresh fish of your choice is delicious in this easy-to-make recipe. Serves 4.

2 tsp. butter **or** margarine
2 Tbsp. minced shallots **or** onions
1¼ lbs. halibut, cod **or** salmon steaks **or** filets
⅛ tsp. lemon herb seasoning
⅛ tsp. white pepper
2 Tbsp. mayonnaise
1 Tbsp.**LEMON** *or* **LEMON-LIME** *or* **LIME MUSTARD**
2 Tbsp. chopped fresh parsley

Melt butter and sauté shallots in small saucepan until transparent. Spread evenly over bottom of broiler-proof baking dish. Place fish in a single layer over shallots. Sprinkle lemon seasoning and pepper over fish.

In a small bowl, combine the next 3 ingredients; spread over fish. Broil 3″ from heat until fish flakes easily with the touch of a fork, (about 8 to 10 minutes, depending upon thickness of fish). Transfer fish to serving platter and keep warm. Transfer baking dish drippings to sauté pan. Add wine and cook over high heat, about 3 minutes, until liquid is reduced by half. Add mustard and parsley; mix and pour over fish. Serve.

SHRIMP DIJON

A rich, creamy Dijonnaise entrée that's absolutely one of my favorites. Serves 6.

5 Tbsp. butter
4 Tbsp. flour
2 cups milk
½ tsp. dry mustard
⅛ tsp. cayenne
3 Tbsp. shallots, minced
½ cup white wine
¼ cup parsley, minced
1 egg yolk, beaten
3 Tbsp. **LIME, LEMON-LIME, SHALLOT** *or* **HONEY DIJON MUSTARD**
1½ lbs. large shrimp, washed, shelled and deveined
½ cup Parmesan cheese, grated

Preheat oven to 450°F. Over medium heat, melt 3 tablespoons butter in saucepan; stir in flour (make a roux). Reduce heat to low and stir constantly for several minutes. Gradually add milk, stirring constantly. Add mustard and cayenne; simmer 15 minutes, stirring occasionally. Add shallots, wine and parsley; simmer 10 minutes, stirring occasionally. Add 2 tablespoons of this sauce to beaten egg yolk, stirring quickly. Then add yolk mixture to remainder of sauce while stirring constantly.

Sauté shrimp in remaining butter about 3 minutes, until opaque. Remove shrimp, drain butter and replace shrimp in pan. Add about a third of the sauce; mix. Spoon into 4 individual ovenproof dishes, cover with remaining sauce and sprinkle with cheese. Bake 15 minutes.

IMPRESSIVE CRAB

An absolutely elegant entrée! Serves 8.

1 green pepper, minced
1 medium onion, minced
1 tsp. dry mustard
2 Tbsp. **HERBES DE PROVENCE** *or*
  HORSERADISH LOVERS MUSTARD
2 tsp. prepared horseradish (optional)
2 tsp. white pepper
2 eggs, beaten
1 cup mayonnaise
3 lbs. real **or** imitation crab meat
¾ lb. Swiss **or** Parmesan cheese, grated, **or** a
  combination of both

Preheat oven to 350° F. Combine first 7 ingredients;
mix well. Blend in mayonnaise, then crab meat. Spoon
mixture evenly into 8 individual ovenproof serving
dishes. Sprinkle with cheeses. Arrange dishes on
baking pan, and bake in preheated oven for 20
minutes, until heated through and cheese browned.

POULET MOUTARDE DIJONNAISE HELENE

*A simple and expandable recipe for "**Helene's
Chicken with Dijon-style Mustard**", done in the
French manner. Use any of the flavored Dijon-style
mustards in this book.*

chicken pieces of choice
cooking oil of choice
ANY DIJON-STYLE MUSTARD
dry white wine
fresh bread crumbs

Brush chicken pieces with oil and broil on each side.
Combine equal parts mustard and wine. Brush chicken
with mustard mixture and sprinkle with bread crumbs.
Broil until browned. Serve.

CHICKEN TARRAGON

The flavors are just superb in this company-perfect dish. Serves 8.

1 lb. fresh mushrooms, washed and sliced
2 Tbsp. butter **or** margarine
8 chicken breasts, skinned and boned
2 Tbsp. butter **or** margarine
2 Tbsp. oil
6 shallots, chopped
2 carrots, sliced in 1/2″ rounds
¼ cup cognac or brandy
1 cup dry white wine
¼ cup fresh tarragon or 2 Tbsp. dried tarragon leaves
1½ Tbsp. fresh chervil, chopped **or** ½ tsp. dried
  chervil
1 tsp. salt
1 tsp. white pepper
1 cup half and half **or** light cream
3 Tbsp. **TARRAGON MUSTARD**
1 egg yolk
1 Tbsp. flour

In a dutch oven or large saucepan sauté mushrooms in 2 tablespoons butter until tender. Set aside. Next sauté chicken in butter and oil, browning on each side. Set chicken aside. Add shallots and carrots to drippings in pan; sauté for 5 minutes. Return chicken to pan; add cognac, wine, tarragon, chervil, salt and pepper. Bring to a boil then reduce heat, simmering covered for 30 minutes.

In a small bowl, combine half and half, mustard, egg yolks and flour. Remove chicken to heated platter, keep warm. Strain drippings in pan, discarding solids. Return drippings to pan. Mix cream mixture into drippings. Cook over medium heat, adding a little wine if sauce seems too thick. Spoon sauce and mushrooms over chicken. Serve.

OMAHA CHICKEN

I doubt that Omaha has heard of this dish. When I first started making this, it was developed from an Italian dish that I could not pronounce. So, my best friend, Robert, nicknamed it, and it still remains our favorite chicken dish. Serves 4.

4 chicken breasts, skinned, boned and sliced
   horizontally to make 8 thin slices
1 cup flour with 1 tsp. dry mustard, mixed
3 Tbsp. butter **or** margarine
2 Tbsp. oil
LIME *or* LEMON-LIME MUSTARD
8 thin 2"x4" slices of prosciutto ham
8 thin 2"x4" slices Bel Paese cheese
¼ cup freshly grated Parmesan cheese

Preheat oven to 350° F. Lay chicken strips on a piece of wax paper, cover with another sheet of wax paper. Pound chicken lightly to flatten pieces. Remove wax paper. Put flour mixture into shallow bowl, dredge chicken strips through flour and shake off excess.

In a heavy skillet, saute chicken in butter and oil over medium heat until golden brown. (Be careful not to overcook.)

Place chicken in a single layer, in a baking dish. Brush a very thin coat of mustard on each piece of chicken. Top with prosciutto and cheese slices. Sprinkle with Parmesan. Bake about 10 minutes, uncovered, until cheese melts and is lightly browned.

HONEY GLAZED CHICKEN

*Quick and easy to prepare. A light and piquant
chicken dish. Serves 4.*

2 tbsp. butter
juice of 1 lemon
¼ cup honey
¾ tsp. salt
½ tsp. dry mustard
grated peel of lemon
2 Tbsp. **LEMON, HOT SWEDISH STYLE, SWEET
'N' HOT, LEMON THYME, HONEY DIJON** *or*
SHALLOT MUSTARD
4 chicken breasts

Preheat oven to 350°F. Melt butter in small saucepan;
add next 6 ingredients and mix well over low heat. Dip
chicken into glaze, coat both sides, place in baking
dish. Pour remaining sauce over chicken and bake in
oven for 45 minutes; turn chicken over and bake
another 15 minutes. Serve.

Variations: LIME-HONEY GLAZED CHICKEN:
Omit lemon juice and peel, instead add juice of 1
lime, grated lime peel and use **LIME MUSTARD.**

ORANGE-HONEY GLAZED CHICKEN: Omit
lemon juice and peel, instead add juice of ½ orange,
grated peel of ½ orange and use **ORANGE
MUSTARD.**

FRUITED-HONEY GLAZED CHICKEN: Omit
lemon juice and peel, instead add ½ cup crushed
pineapple, 1 tsp. Worcestershire sauce and use
APRICOT MUSTARD.

MARINATED CHICKEN

This is perfect hot weather fare. Start the barbecue and enjoy this light and low-calorie entrée. This recipe may be baked if you prefer. About 120 calories per serving. Serves 4.

½ cup soy sauce
½ cup raspberry vinegar **or** other vinegar of choice
½ cup red wine, (optional)
2 Tbsp. fresh grated ginger
2 cloves garlic, pressed
2 Tbsp. **ANY DIJON-STYLE MUSTARD**
½ tsp. curry
1 Tbsp. dry mustard
4 (1 lb.) skinned and boned chicken breasts

Combine the first 8 ingredients in a large bowl. Place chicken in marinade mixture, cover. Marinate 6 or more hours. Barbecue or bake in a 350° F oven for 1 hour.

LEMON CHICKEN

This dish goes together quickly for those busy days we all have. Tastes great and is low-calorie too, about 120 calories per serving. Serves 4.

1 tsp. lemon herb seasoning
juice of ½ fresh lemon
grated peel of ½ lemon
2 Tbsp. **LEMON MUSTARD**
½ tsp. white pepper
4 (1 lb.) skinned chicken breasts, boned if you prefer

Preheat oven to 350° F. Place chicken in baking dish. Combine first 5 ingredients in small bowl. Pour mixture over chicken. Bake for 1 hour.

MUSTARD SPARERIBS

This is a summer favorite. Easy to make for hot weather cooking. Serves 8.

4 lbs. spareribs, cut into serving size pieces
1 cup chopped onions
2 cloves garlic, chopped
1 cup fresh mushrooms, sliced **or** minced
¼ cup oil
2 Tbsp. red wine vinegar
2 Tbsp. honey
¼ cup lime juice
grated peel of lime
3 Tbsp. **LIME MUSTARD**
2 tsp. each salt and pepper
¼ cup soy sauce
⅔ cup red wine
½ cup chili sauce

Sauté onions, garlic and mushrooms in oil until tender. Add remaining ingredients, mix well. Baste spareribs with mixture.

Barbecue on grill until done. Spareribs may also be baked in a 325°F. oven for 1 hour. Baste frequently with either method.

Variation: Substitute lemon juice and peel for lime. Substitute your favorite mustard (**HERB MUSTARDS** work especially well) for the **LIME MUSTARD.**

MARINATED PORK CHOPS WITH CRANBERRY MUSTARD SAUCE

The mustard and red wine vinegar marinade is the base for this tangy sauce. An excellent make ahead dish. Serves 6.

6 – 1½" thick pork chops
salt and pepper, to taste
½ cup **ORANGE, LIME, LEMON, HONEY DIJON, RED WINE, CHAMPAGNE, HOT SWEDISH STYLE** *or* **APRICOT MUSTARD**
1 cup red wine vinegar
¼ cup butter or margarine
¼ cup chopped shallots
2 Tbsp. flour
2 Tbsp. chicken broth
3 Tbsp. whole cranberry sauce
1 Tbsp. chopped parsley

Place pork chops in shallow dish. Season with salt and pepper. Mix mustard and vinegar; pour over pork chops. Cover and marinate overnight.

Preheat oven to 425°F. Brown drained pork chops in butter, remove from pan and saute shallots. Stir in flour and chicken broth; when thickened add remaining ingredients. Pour mixture over chops and bake for 20 minutes.

CARAWAY CHEESE POTATOES

This Swiss-style potato dish will be a "request" recipe. Serves 6.

3 large new potatoes, boiled, cooled and cubed
5 Tbsp. butter
⅓ cup green onions, thinly sliced
3 Tbsp. flour
1½ cup chicken broth
1 tsp. caraway seed
½ tsp. cumin powder
salt and white pepper, to taste
1 cup shredded Swiss cheese
½ cup fresh bread crumbs, coarse
⅛ tsp. paprika
3 tbsp. **HERBES DE PROVENCE** *or* **HOT SWEDISH STYLE** *or* **SWEET 'N' HOT MUSTARD**

Place cubed potatoes in a 2-quart casserole. In saucepan, melt butter, set aside 2 tablespoons, add onions and sauté until transparent. Add flour and cook until bubbly. Add broth, caraway, cumin and mustard. Cook until thickened. Pour over potatoes. Spread cheese on top and sprinkle bread crumbs, paprika and remainder of butter on top. Bake uncovered at 400 F. for 20 minutes.

SESAME BROCCOLI

Serve this with **MARINATED CHICKEN** *for a light Oriental-style meal that is under 250 calories per serving! Served alone this dish is about 50 calories per serving. Serves 4.*

1 lb. cooked broccoli spears
1 Tbsp. salad oil
1 Tbsp. vinegar, flavor of choice
1 Tbsp. soy sauce
1 Tbsp. **ANY DIJON-STYLE MUSTARD**
4 tsp sugar
1 Tbsp. toasted sesame seeds

Place cooked broccoli in serving dish. Combine all remaining ingredients in saucepan. Stir and bring to a boil. Pour over spears, turn to coat evenly. Serve.

LEEKS VINAIGRETTE

Need something a little extraordinaire? Here leeks star as a cold side dish, instead of hot. Serves 6.

12 leeks
3 whole cloves
2 cups dry white wine

Vinaigrette:

2 Tbsp. **TARRAGON MUSTARD** *or* **HOT SWEDISH MUSTARD**
2 tsp. salt
½ tsp. fresh pepper
¼ tsp. sugar
¼ cup tarragon vinegar **or** apple cider vinegar
1 cup oil
2 Tbsp. fresh **or** 1 Tbsp. dried tarragon **or** parsley

Wash and trim leeks to 6″ above white part. Split in half to 1″ above root ends, not allowing leeks to separate completely. Combine cloves and wine in saucepan; bring to a boil. Reduce heat, add leeks and poach gently 5 to 8 minutes. Drain, transfer to shallow bowl, cover and refrigerate.

Prepare vinaigrette by combining mustard, salt, pepper and sugar in blender. Add vinegar and continue blending. Add oil in a steady stream while blending. When liquid has thickened, add tarragon and mix 3 or 4 seconds more. (Vinaigrette may be made up to a week in advance.)

To serve, arrange leeks on platter and pour vinaigrette over, serving remainder of dressing separately.

HORSERADISH MUSTARD SAUCE

Serve this sauce with corned beef and listen to the compliments! Makes about ¾ cup.

2 Tbsp. prepared horseradish
2 Tbsp. white wine vinegar
2 Tbsp. **LIME, TARRAGON** *or* **HORSERADISH LOVERS MUSTARD**
dash of cayenne
½ cup whipping cream

Combine all ingredients except whipping cream in a small bowl. Whip cream to soft peaks, fold into mustard mixture. Serve. Refrigerate any leftover sauce.

SUPERB MUSTARD COATING FOR HAM

A different topping for ham that has always been a real hit. Easy and elegant! This topping is added to your ham in its last 20 minutes of baking time. Makes about ½ cup, enough for a 6-lb. ham.

2 Tbsp. dry mustard
½ Tbsp. cornstarch
1 egg yolk
1 Tbsp. **LIME, APRICOT, SWEET 'N' HOT, ORANGE,** *or* **HONEY DIJON MUSTARD**
fine fresh bread crumbs

Mix all ingredients except bread crumbs together. Remove ham from oven in its last 20 minutes of cooking time. Spread mustard coating on top and sides. Sprinkle bread crumbs over. Return to oven and bake for 20 minutes.

ZINGY MUSTARD SAUCE

This is an eye opener as well as a taste tingler. Serve with roast beef. Makes about ¾ cup.

2 egg yolks
2 Tbsp. **HERBES DE PROVENCE, BAVARIAN BROWN** *or* **GREEN PEPPERCORN MUSTARD**
1 Tbsp. prepared horseradish
1 Tbsp. sugar
2 Tbsp. wine vinegar
1 Tbsp. white wine
1 Tbsp. butter **or** margarine
½ tsp. salt
½ cup whipping cream

Combine all ingredients except whipping cream in a small saucepan, mix well. Cook over low heat until sauce thickens, about 2 minutes. Remove from heat, stir until smooth and cool. Whip cream and fold into cooled mixture. Serve. Refrigerate any leftover sauce.

CREAMY MUSTARD SAUCE

A quick and easy party dip for all "dippables". Especially good as a sauce with meat or vegetable fondues. Does not keep, so serve immediately. Makes 1 cup.

2 Tbsp. **ANY DIJON-BASED MUSTARD** from this book
1 Tbsp. dry mustard
1 cup whipping cream, whipped into soft peaks

Combine mustards into a smooth paste. Gently fold mustards into whipped cream until just blended. Serve immediately.

55

LIME SAUCE

This is, without a doubt, my favorite sauce for baked or poached fish. Wonderful on baked halibut, grilled salmon or stuffed sole. Makes about 1 cup.

2 Tbsp. butter
2 shallots, minced
¾ cup white wine (Chardonnay is best)
1 cup heavy cream
1 Tbsp. **LIME MUSTARD**

Over medium heat, melt butter in sautépan. Sauté shallots until transparent. Add wine and cook until volume is reduced by half. Turn heat to low, then add cream slowly, stirring constantly until volume is reduced by half. Add mustard. Serve immediately.

FRENCH MUSTARD SAUCE

This is hot stuff! This special sauce, rather like a Chinese hot mustard, is great with roast beef or pork, hot dogs or sausage. Makes ½ cup.

½ cup dry mustard
¼ cup beer
½ tsp. salt
1 Tbsp. red wine vinegar

Mix all ingredients in a bowl.

CREOLE REMOULADE SAUCE

A perfect sauce for shrimp or crab cocktail. Makes about 4 cups.

3 Tbsp. capers, drained
1½ tsp. hot sauce
½ cup parsley, chopped
¼ cup green onions, chopped
¾ cup celery, minced
¼ cup lemon juice
¼ cup catsup
½ cup **GREEN PEPPERCORN, BAVARIAN BROWN, HOT SWEDISH-STYLE, HORSERADISH LOVERS** *or* any ⌐IJON-BASED **MUSTARD**
1 Tbsp. prepared horseradish
1 Tbsp. Worcestershire sauce
2 cups mayonnaise

Combine all ingredients and refrigerate until well chilled. Serve cold.

HERMITS

This recipe provides a different twist to an old-fashioned drop cookie favorite. Makes about 4 dozen cookies.

2¼ cups flour
1 tsp. baking soda
¼ tsp. salt
¾ tsp. allspice
¾ tsp. cinnamon
½ tsp. cloves
½ tsp. dry mustard
½ cup shortening
1 cup honey
½ cup brown sugar, packed
1 tsp. **HOT SWEDISH-STYLE MUSTARD**
2 eggs, beaten
3 Tbsp. milk
1 cup dried currants
1 cup dates, chopped
½ cup chopped nuts, (walnuts, pecans, etc.)

Preheat oven to 400°F. Sift together the first 7 ingredients. Cream the next 4 ingredients together in large bowl. Add eggs to creamed mixture. Add milk and sifted dry ingredients, mix well. Stir in fruits and nuts. Drop from teaspoon onto a lightly greased baking sheet. Bake for 10 to 12 minutes.

SPICED CHOCOLATE CAKE

This has been one of the most used recipes in my collection. Try it, and you'll see why it's so popular. Extra moist, so it needs no frosting unless you wish. Great packed for lunches! Makes one 9"x13" sheet cake.

½ cup butter or margarine, softened
½ cup oil
1¾ cups sugar
2 eggs
1½ tsp. vanilla
½ cup sour milk
1 tsp. **HOT SWEDISH-STYLE MUSTARD**
2½ cups flour
4 Tbsp. cocoa, (heaping tablespoons)
½ tsp. baking powder
1 tsp. cinnamon
1 tsp. cloves
1 tsp. dry mustard
2 cups zucchini, finely diced **or** shredded
¾ cup chocolate chips

Preheat oven to 325°F. Cream first 3 ingredients together, then add next 4 ingredients, mix well with mixer. Combine together the next 7 dry ingredients and add to creamed mixture. Stir in zucchini and half of the chocolate chips. Pour mixture into prepared 9"x13"x2" baking pan. Sprinkle remaining chocolate chips over top. Bake for 40 to 45 minutes or until toothpick comes out clean. No need to frost, it is so moist. Serve warm or cooled.

INDEX

Appetizers

Desserts

Entrées, Meats, Poultry and Seafood

61

Soups

Vegetables

"We may live without poetry, music and art;
We may live without conscience, and live
  without heart;
We may live without friends; we may
  live without books;
But civilized man cannot live
  without cooks."

Owen Meredith

BOOK ORDER FORM

CULINARY ARTS LTD.
Publishers of Fine Specialty Cookbooks
P.O. Box 2157, Lake Oswego, Oregon 97035   (503) 639-4549

☐ **Gourmet Mustards: How To Make And Cook With Them**
By Helene Sawyer
This 64-page softcover cookbook is indexed.
ISBN# 0-914667-07-6 (paperbound) $4.95
ISBN# 0-914667-09-2 (combbound) $5.95

☐ **How To Make And Cook With Gourmet Vinegars**
By Marsha Peters Johnson
This 64-page softcover cookbook is indexed.
ISBN# 0-914667-05-X (paperbound) $4.95

☐ **How To Make Danish Fruit Liqueurs**
By Cheryl Long
This 80-page softcover cookbook is indexed.
ISBN# 0-914667-03-3 (paperbound) $5.95

☐ **How To Make A World Of Liqueurs**
By Heather Kibbey and Cheryl Long
This 96-page cookbook is indexed.
ISBN# 0-914667-02-5 (paperbound) $6.95

Please send: Vinegar _____

Mustard (paperbound) _____   World _____

Mustard (combbound) _____   Danish _____

Check/money order $_____

[MasterCard] #_____   Exp. date _____

[VISA] #_____

Signature _____

Name_____

Address_____

City_____State_____Zip Code_____

Shipping: Add $1.00 for postage and handling.   63